Home-made
Chocolates &
Truffles

Home-made
Chocolates &
Truffles

25 traditional recipes for shaped, filled &
hand-dipped confections

Claire Ptak

LORENZ BOOKS

This edition is published by
Lorenz Books, an imprint of
Anness Publishing Ltd,
108 Great Russell Street
London WC1B 3NA

info@anness.com

www.lorenzbooks.com;
www.annesspublishing.com

If you like the images in this book
and would like to investigate using
them for publishing, promotions or
advertising, please visit our website
www.practicalpictures.com for
more information.

© Anness Publishing Ltd 2014

A CIP catalogue record for this book is
available from the British Library.

Publisher: *Joanna Lorenz*
Editor: *Kate Eddison, Helen Sudell*
Photographer: *Nicki Dowey*
Food Stylist: *Claire Ptak*
Food Stylist's Assistants: *Kate
  McCullough* and *Adriana Nascimento*
Prop Stylists: *Wei Tang* and
  Marianne de Vries
Designer: *Lisa Tai*
Production Controller: *Pirong Wang*

COOK'S NOTES
- Bracketed terms are intended for American readers.
- For all recipes, quantities are given in both metric and imperial measures and, where appropriate, in standard cups and spoons. Follow one set of measures, but not a mixture, because they are not interchangeable.
- Standard spoon and cup measures are level. 1 tsp = 5ml, 1 tbsp = 15ml, 1 cup = 250ml/8fl oz.
- Australian standard tablespoons are 20ml. Australian readers should use 3 tsp in place of 1 tbsp for measuring small quantities.
- American pints are 16fl oz/2 cups. American readers should use 20fl oz/2.5 cups in place of 1 pint when measuring liquids.
- Electric oven temperatures in this book are for conventional ovens. When using a fan oven, the temperature will probably need to be reduced by about 10–20°C/20–40°F. Since ovens vary, you should check with your manufacturer's instruction book for guidance.
- The nutritional analysis given for each recipe, unless otherwise stated, is calculated per portion (i.e. serving or item).
  The analysis does not include optional ingredients, such as salt added to taste.
- Medium (US large) eggs are used unless otherwise stated.

Front cover image shows Ceylon Cinnamon Truffles, for recipe see page 26

PUBLISHER'S NOTE

Previously published as part of a larger volume, *The Complete Guide to Making Sweets, Candy & Chocolates.*

Contents

Introduction

Think Valentine's Day. Think Easter. Think Christmas. Think chocolate. What better way to celebrate these holidays than with a selection of home-made chocolate confections? Ganache-filled truffles are simple to make and lend themselves to flavourful partnerships. Even easier is a nutty bark that can be broken into bitesize pieces.

Types of chocolate

Chocolate and its powdered version, cocoa, come in so many varieties that the choice can be bewildering. However, there is one simple rule: choose the best quality you can find when buying chocolate for your recipes. It will make a huge difference to the end result.

Forms of chocolate vary and the different shapes and sizes fulfil every sweet-maker's requirements. Large blocks of chocolate for cooking are available at fine food stores and online, and some stores are also beginning to stock good chocolate, such as Valrhona and Callebaut, in large blocks. These large blocks are ideal for grating or chopping up finely.

In addition to large blocks and bars, chocolate for sweet-making comes in the form of beans, lozenges, pastilles or drops (chips). Chocolate beans are small individual pieces of chocolate that make measuring and melting easy. These small pieces need to be chopped even more finely with a large cook's knife for tempering.

Chocolate varieties depend on the percentage of pure chocolate in the mix. The recipes in this book suggest a specific percentage of chocolate, and while these are

Above: Plain (semisweet), white and milk chocolate lozenges make measuring out specific quantities easier.

helpful guides, the best way to appreciate a particular chocolate's idiosyncrasies is to taste it for yourself and decide how strong in taste you want your chocolate to be. If a recipe calls for dark (bittersweet) chocolate, for example, decide whether you prefer a 64 percent or a 70 percent variety. Understanding the percentage of the different ingredients in each type of chocolate will also help in deciding which kind to select for particular recipes in this book. General guidelines are given below to help you achieve success.

If a recipe calls for milk chocolate, it is never advisable to substitute dark (bittersweet) chocolate, as they will perform differently in the recipe.

Cooking (unsweetened) chocolate is simple, unadulterated chocolate mass or liquor formed into a bar, with no other ingredients added. It is sometimes known as baking chocolate. It is very bitter in taste, and is not suitable for eating on its own. It works well in certain cake, brownie and confectionery recipes when it is used with sugar, as it imparts a deep and rich chocolate flavour. If wrapped well and stored in a cool, dry place, it will last for a few years.

Dark (bittersweet) chocolate is a combination of cocoa solids, cocoa butter and sugar. The amount of cocoa solids should be at least 55 per cent, but the finest ones are around 64–70 per cent. This is the recommended range to work with for the full-flavoured chocolate sweets and confections presented in this book.

Plain (semisweet) chocolate, like dark (bittersweet) chocolate, is a combination of cocoa solids, cocoa butter and sugar. In this case, the cocoa solids should be at least 15 per cent, but generally they contain 35–55 per cent cocoa solids. Using anything below 35 per cent is not recommended for the recipes in this book, unless a milk or white chocolate is required.

Milk chocolate is a combination of cocoa solids, cocoa butter and sugar, plus at least 12 per cent added milk or cream. In this case, the cocoa solids should be at least 10 per cent and can be as high as 45 per cent. Milk chocolates have improved greatly in recent years, and it is worth trying some of the new ones on the market, which contain higher percentages of cocoa solids.

White chocolate does not contain any cocoa solids at all, and therefore is often not classed as chocolate in a true sense. It consists of a combination of at least 20 per cent cocoa butter, sugar and milk,

Above: Melted chocolate should have a luxuriously smooth consistency.

Above: White chocolate is often used to decorate cakes and desserts.

with no cocoa mass. The milk element should be at least 14 per cent. Today, there are some very flavourful white chocolates on the market, and so it is definitely a variety of chocolate that is worth experimenting with.

Unsweetened cocoa powder has a distinctively bitter taste on its own, but mixed into cakes, biscuits (cookies) and sweets with added sugar, it is magically transformed. Cocoa powder also makes a delicious and attractive topping when dusted lightly over cakes, cookies and truffles as an alternative to, or in addition to, icing (confectioners') sugar.

Chocolate-making Equipment

Although chocolate making is a simple process it is true that a few essential pieces of cooking equipment will make making chocolate at home much easier. Many of the items listed are common kitchen items, and you may only need to invest in a few extra utensils to get started.

A collection of heatproof bowls in varying sizes is practical for melting chocolate and for many other mixing processes. Pretty, stacking ceramic bowls look lovely, but stainless-steel ones have the advantage of being lightweight and cool. A wire rack has many uses in the kitchen.

Ladles, spatulas and spoons are vital pieces of equipment. A ladle will help with delicate operations such as pouring chocolate into moulds. A rubber

Above: Dipping forks.

spatula is essential for mixing and scraping bowls; the best ones are heat-resistant. Thin metal spatulas are ideal for lifting confections from baking sheets or coaxing sweets out of baking tins (pans).

A wire balloon whisk is useful for gently mixing chocolate as it melts, and for combining chocolate and cream in a ganache. A fine-mesh sieve (strainer) is vital for sifting dry ingredients.

Specialist chocolate dipping forks can be used to dip prepared ganache into tempered chocolate, or to mark a pattern on the top of each coated chocolate truffle.

It is possible to make your own piping (pastry) bags out of paper, but a good quality cloth bag (preferably with a plastic coating) or disposable plastic ones are very useful. There is a great choice of nozzles (tips), couplers and bags

at cookware stores. Squeeze bottles are also invaluable for accurate filling of moulds and paper cups.

Clear plastic chocolate moulds sold in most cake-decorating stores are generally considered to be disposable. Once used, they can be very carefully washed with soapy water and a soft cloth, but any scrapes and scratches that remain will appear on the surface

Above: Plastic chocolate moulds.

of the next batch of chocolates. Serious chocolate-makers should invest in some professional reusable chocolate moulds.

There are several different kinds of baking paper available. Baking parchment is usually the most appropriate for oven use; silicone paper is more expensive and even more non-stick than parchment. There are also reusable liners on the market. These should be kept flat or rolled; to clean them, wash with warm soapy water and dry well. Disposable sweet cases are available in many different colours and patterns, and also come in tiny versions that are perfect for truffles.

Special chocolate thermometers measure the lower melting point of chocolate, and they are helpful in achieving a glossy finish.

A domestic chocolate-tempering machine is a fairly expensive piece of equipment, but if you plan on making a lot of truffles it might be a good investment. Tempering gives chocolate a smooth, glossy, professional-looking finish.

Finally, digital scales are a must. They give very accurate readings and will ensure absolute precision when measuring the tiny quantities that are required of certain ingredients in the recipes that follow.

Using chocolate moulds

Chocolate moulds mean you can create your own professional-looking chocolates using tempered chocolate.

1 Coat the cups with tempered chocolate. Tilt the mould over a clean bowl so the chocolate runs down and coats the inside of the cups, with the excess drizzling into the bowl.

2 Using a large palette knife, scrape away any excess chocolate from the flat plastic surrounding the cups. Allow the chocolate to set completely then fill with your chosen filling.

3 The next day temper a little more chocolate and pour over the set filling. Scrape any excess chocolate off the top (which will be the bottom of the chocolates) and leave to set for 1-1½ hours.

Preparing Chocolate

Chocolate can be an intimidating ingredient. Words such as split, separate, break, bloom and seize are often associated with its preparation. What is more, there is the percentage of cocoa bean solids to consider and which brands to choose from. So before you start to get creative, take a little time to learn the basics that will help in achieving chocolate success.

Buying chocolate

It is possible to buy professional chocolate in pellets (also called beans or pastilles, depending on the manufacturer). The pellets are easier to measure and use and save time on chopping. But the large blocks are ideal for making chocolate curls, and they are less expensive to buy.

Above: A block of good quality French milk chocolate.

Chopping chocolate

It is best to use a heavy chef's knife to chop blocks of chocolate. If it is a very large block, break it into smaller pieces first.

1 Starting at one corner and on a cooled chopping board, chop the chocolate with a large, heavy knife, using your non-dominant hand to hold the tip of the knife down.

2 Once you have chopped all the way along, turn the board 90° and repeat until all the chocolate is chopped finely.

Melting chocolate

Many recipes in this book will require melted chocolate. Although, for speed, you can melt chocolate in a microwave, by far the best method is described here. When melting chocolate, all equipment must be completely dry. Do not cover during or after melting because any water or condensation could cause the chocolate to seize and stiffen.

Grating chocolate

It is a good idea to chill chocolate before grating, to stop it melting in your hands.

1 Use a box grater to grate the chocolate, using different sides for different effects. Transfer the grated chocolate to a bowl and chill until needed.

1 If you are using a block of chocolate, break it into small pieces. Place the chocolate in a heatproof bowl and set it above a pan of barely simmering water. Do not let the water touch the bottom of the bowl.

2 Allow the chocolate to melt over a gentle heat, stirring occasionally, until it has a smooth consistency. Remove from the heat and stir.

Storing Chocolate

Freshly made chocolates are best served immediately, or stored in an airtight container, spaced apart, in the refrigerator. Remove 30 minutes before serving, as chocolate should be eaten at room temperature.

12

Tempering Chocolate

To get a professional shine and finish on your chocolates, you need to temper the chocolate. This means heating and cooling it to specific temperatures in order to make the crystals in the chocolate align in a certain way. You will need a chocolate thermometer for accurate readings.

How to temper chocolate

Different types of chocolates temper at varying temperatures, so find out which chocolate is right for the recipe and use the chart below.

It is vital to use a special chocolate thermometer, which records very low temperatures. All melting should be done in a heatproof bowl over a pan of barely simmering water, and the bottom of the bowl should not touch the water. The heat may not need to be turned on again for the second melting as the water beneath may still be hot enough to melt the mixture. Never walk away from chocolate while it is being tempered as variations in the air temperature can affect the rate of melting from one day to the next. If the tempered chocolate becomes too firm, warm it again, but do not exceed the final reheating temperature for the type of chocolate you are using.

Cook's Tip

Some recipes call for just a small amount of tempered chocolate, but it is easier to temper at least 300g/10½oz of chocolate and it is not recommended to try tempering less than this. If the particular recipe you are following does not need all the tempered chocolate, simply pour it out on to a piece of baking parchment and leave it to set. This chocolate can then be recycled into brownies, cakes, cookies or any recipe where the chocolate will be cooked and does not need to have a shiny finish. Whatever you do, do not waste it!

Tempering Temperature Chart

Type of chocolate	First melt to:	Cool to:	Melt again to:
Dark (bittersweet)	40–46°C/ 104–115°F	27–28°C/ 80–82°F	31–32°C/ 88–89°F
Milk	32.5°C/ 90°F	27–28°C/ 80–82°F	30°C/ 86°F
White	30.5°C/ 87°F	27°C/ 80°F	28°C/ 82°F

1 Place two-thirds of the chopped chocolate or pellets in a heatproof bowl over a pan of barely simmering water, making sure no water touches the bottom of the bowl and no steam or water ever comes into contact with the chocolate.

2 Use a chocolate thermometer to melt the chocolate to the 'first melt to' temperature on the chart opposite. When the chocolate has almost melted to this temperature, remove the bowl and place it on a folded dish towel.

3 Stir the chocolate once with a wooden spoon or heatproof spatula. Stir in a spoonful of the remaining third of the chocolate. This additional chocolate is known as the 'seed' chocolate.

4 Once the first spoonful of the seed chocolate has melted in, add another spoonful and stir until it has melted completely. Continue in this way until the seed chocolate no longer melts when added, then stop adding the seed chocolate.

5 Allow the chocolate to continue to cool down on its own. Check with a chocolate thermometer when it reaches the 'cool to' temperature on the chart. This should take about 10–15 minutes. Do not stop watching the thermometer.

6 Reheat the chocolate to the third temperature on the chart. Bring it back up to this higher temperature by placing the bowl back over the pan. Be very careful at this stage not to overheat it. The chocolate is now ready for use.

Making Ganache

Ganache is a mixture of chocolate, cream and butter, and is a wonderfully versatile paste. It can be infused with many flavours, and the ganache can become the creamy centre of a chocolate-coated truffle, or form the entire truffle itself. While warm, ganache is often poured over cakes, but once it has begun to set, it is excellent for decorative piping.

Above: A creamy ganache centre is the perfect filling for a whole host of home-made chocolates.

Flavouring ganache

Among the best ingredients to flavour ganache, try vanilla, cinnamon, orange and coffee. For adults, brandy, champagne and rum are all excellent.

Infusing ganache

If the recipe calls for an infused cream to flavour the ganache, leave the cream to infuse in the refrigerator with the flavouring before straining and warming it. Taste it before heating the cream – it should taste slightly too strong. When the cream is whisked into the chocolate, the flavour will then be diluted.

How to make ganache

The two most important things to consider when making ganache are mixing and temperature. The temperature must be controlled – a chocolate thermometer that shows very low temperatures is essential for making ganache.

Makes 60–100 truffles

350g/12oz dark (bittersweet) chocolate (66–70% cocoa solids), chopped

120ml/4fl oz/½ cup double (heavy) cream

50g/2oz/4 tbsp unsalted butter, softened (it needs to be very soft)

1 Melt the dark chocolate in a heatproof bowl over a pan of barely simmering water (see page 13) to 46°C/115°F on a chocolate thermometer.

2 Meanwhile, gently warm the cream to the same temperature in a separate pan and then pour the warmed cream over the melted chocolate.

Piping ganache truffles

A number of recipes require piped truffles, so follow the instructions below to create chilled, firm truffles. Allow the ganache to set enough to hold its shape, but not so hard that it is difficult to work with. When the ganache is at the desired consistency for piping, spoon a small amount into a piping (pastry) bag fitted with a suitable nozzle. The heat from your hands may cause the ganache to melt, so work quickly in small batches.

3 Mix them together into a silky mass with a hand blender or wire whisk. If the ganache separates, it can sometimes be salvaged with the addition of a small amount of warmed cream. Add the very soft butter, bit by bit, blending well between each addition.

4 Transfer the mixture to a square cake tin (pan) lined with clear film (plastic wrap). If the ganache cools in a round bowl, the sides can harden before the centre, causing lumps to form. Allow the ganache to set at room temperature until it begins to firm up.

1 Using a piping bag fitted with a large round nozzle, pipe even-sized blobs on to a baking sheet lined with baking parchment. Place in the refrigerator for about 20 minutes, or until firm, then roll each blob into a ball in your hands. Chill for 10 minutes, until firm.

Making Truffles

Once you have mastered the art of making ganache, you are ready to turn the ganache into delectable truffles. Truffles can be simple or luxurious, often containing alcohol or other flavourings. They can be dusted in cocoa powder or coated with tempered chocolate. If you can bear to part with them, they also make lovely gifts!

Shaping truffles

Truffles can be spherical or square. First of all make the ganache following the method on pages 14–15 and let it cool at room temperature for a couple of hours, then in the refrigerator until firm. Once set, turn the ganache out on to a board. Once shaped, truffles will keep for approximately 3 weeks in the refrigerator or up to 2 months in the freezer.

Simple round truffles

1 Cut the ganache into truffle-sized squares – this quantity should make 60–100 truffles depending on how big you make the squares. Prepare a bowl of unsweetened cocoa powder and dust your hands with it.

2 Take the squares one by one and roll them into balls between your cocoa powder-dusted palms. Place on a baking parchment-lined baking tray. You can shape them into more rustic shapes, if you like.

3 Roll the truffles in another layer of cocoa powder and serve immediately or store them in an airtight container dusted with extra cocoa powder, in the refrigerator. Remove the truffles 30 minutes before serving.

Dipping truffles

The next step in the hierarchy of truffles is the dipped version. Dipping chocolate truffles into tempered chocolate will result in a lovely, smooth finish. It also gives a surprising texture, as the crisp outer shell of tempered chocolate gives way to a creamy ganache centre. For round truffles, follow the shaping steps opposite, but instead of rolling them in unsweetened cocoa powder, use a dipping fork to dip them into tempered chocolate and then place them on a baking tray lined with baking parchment or a wire rack to set.

Square dipped truffles

1 To cut the ready-made ganache into truffle-sized squares, remove the cling film (plastic wrap). Dip a large knife in hot water, wipe it dry and use it to trim off any uneven edges from the ganache block. Then slice the block into 2cm/¾in squares. Return to the refrigerator to chill for a further 30 minutes. Meanwhile, temper the dark (see pages 12-13), milk or white chocolate.

2 Use a dipping fork to dip each square of ganache into the tempered chocolate. Carefully lift the truffles back up and drag the bottom of the fork along the side of the bowl to remove any excess tempered chocolate.

3 Leave them to set on a baking tray lined with baking parchment. If you wish to add any decoration to a dipped truffle, you must do so immediately before the chocolate begins to set.

Cook's tip

Warm hands can spoil truffles. Cool your hands down by clasping some ice in a plastic bag for a few moments. Rubber or latex gloves will also help keep the truffles from melting on the fingers.

The Recipes

If you are fond of chocolates then you will find the following selection of home-made truffles and moulded confections irresistible. Ganache-filled truffles are simple to make and lend themselves to divine flavour combinations. Even easier is a nutty bark that can be broken into bitesize pieces, or a rich creamy chocolate peppermint to hand round after dinner. These gorgeous candies will impress your friends and taste sensational.

Dark Chocolate Truffles

Smooth, creamy and intensely chocolatey, these classic truffles are a truly decadent, grown-up treat. Use the best-quality chocolate you can, as this will really give the truffles an extra-special edge. These are perfect for gifts and look very attractive piled up in a box.

Makes about 100

120ml/4fl oz/½ cup double (heavy) cream

100g/3¾oz golden (light corn) syrup

1 vanilla pod (bean), split in half

350g/12oz dark (bittersweet) chocolate (66–70% cocoa solids), chopped

50g/2oz/¼ cup unsalted butter, softened (it needs to be very soft)

unsweetened cocoa powder, for dusting

Cook's Tip

Here, the truffles are made into rough, rustic shapes. If you prefer, you can roll them into neat balls.

1 Stir the cream and golden syrup together in a heavy pan, then scrape the vanilla seeds out of the pod and add to the pan along with the pod. Warm over low heat and bring to just below the boil.

2 Remove from the heat, transfer to a large heatproof mixing bowl and cover with clear film (plastic wrap). Allow to cool, then chill overnight.

3 Grease a 20cm/8in square baking tin (pan) and line with clear film. Place the chocolate in a heatproof bowl and set it over a pan of barely simmering water. Using a chocolate thermometer, heat the chocolate to just below 46°C/115°F. Remove from the heat.

4 Meanwhile, place the bowl containing the cream and golden syrup mixture over a pan of simmering water, remove and discard the vanilla pod, then heat the cream mixture to just below 46°C/115°F.

5 Once they have both reached the desired temperature, pour the melted chocolate and the heated cream into a blender, and blend until it is thick and creamy. Add the very soft butter, bit by bit, blending well between each addition so it is completely incorporated.

6 Pour the ganache into the prepared baking tin and smooth the surface with an offset spatula. Leave to cool for a few hours until it has set. You can then place it into the refrigerator until you are ready to form the truffles.

7 Dust the truffles with cocoa powder and form the truffles following the instructions on page 16.

8 Serve immediately, or place the truffles in a bag or container with extra cocoa powder (to keep them from sticking together) and store in the refrigerator. Remove from the refrigerator 30 minutes before serving.

Energy 62kcal/256kJ; Protein 0.4g; Carbohydrate 3.6g, of which sugars 3.6g; Fat 5g, of which saturates 3.1g; Cholesterol 9mg; Calcium 4mg; Fibre 0.1g; Sodium 6mg

Burnt Caramel Truffles

The key to getting the sumptuous burnt caramel flavour of these truffles is in the careful cooking of the caramel. It needs to be boiled until dark and rich, but just removed from the heat before it actually burns. These confections make a lovely gift.

Makes about 100

50ml/2fl oz/¼ cup cold water
200g/7oz/1 cup caster
  (superfine) sugar
2.5ml/½ tsp cream of tartar
225ml/7½fl oz/scant 1 cup
  double (heavy) cream
50g/2oz/¼ cup unsalted butter,
  plus extra for greasing
2.5ml/½ tsp sea salt
425g/15oz dark (bittersweet)
  chocolate (70% cocoa solids),
  finely chopped
unsweetened cocoa powder, for
  dusting

1 Grease a 20cm/8in square baking tin (pan) and line with clear film (plastic wrap). Place the water in a heavy pan and add the sugar. Add the cream of tartar and heat gently, stirring, until the sugar has dissolved.

2 Turn the heat up to high and bring to the boil. Boil until a dark caramel forms, taking care not to let it burn. Slowly add the cream to the caramel (it will spatter so use caution). Use a whisk to incorporate it fully. Add the butter and salt, and whisk until smooth.

3 Put the chopped chocolate in a large heatproof bowl. Pour over the caramel. Whisk gently until smooth and melted. Pour into the prepared tin. Leave the mixture to set for a couple of hours at room temperature, then chill until firm.

4 Dust the truffles with cocoa powder and form the truffles following the instructions on page 16.

5 Serve immediately, or place the truffles in a bag or container with extra cocoa powder and store in the refrigerator. Remove from the refrigerator at least 30 minutes before serving.

Energy 89kcal/372kJ; Protein 1g; Carbohydrate 10g, of which sugars 10g; Fat 6g, of which saturates 3g; Cholesterol 9mg; Calcium 6mg; Fibre 0g; Sodium 21mg

Hazelnut Praline Truffles

Chocolate and hazelnuts are a match made in heaven. Toasting the nuts not only brings out the flavour, but it also makes them more crunchy. In this recipe they are then mixed with a light, subtly flavoured caramel and coated in milk chocolate.

Makes about 100

150g/5oz/generous ¾ cup
  hazelnuts
50ml/2fl oz/¼ cup cold water
200g/7oz/1 cup sugar
2.5ml/½ tsp cream of tartar
225ml/8fl oz/1 cup double
  (heavy) cream
50g/2oz/¼ cup unsalted butter,
  plus extra for greasing
425g/15oz dark (bittersweet)
  chocolate, finely chopped
400g/14oz milk chocolate,
  tempered (see pages 12–13)

Cook's Tip
If not serving immediately, store in an airtight container, spaced apart, in the refrigerator and remove 30 minutes before serving.

1 Grease a 20cm/8in square baking tin (pan) and line it with clear film (plastic wrap). Preheat the oven to 180°C/350°F/Gas 4.

2 Toast the hazelnuts on a baking sheet in the oven for about 7 minutes. Allow to cool, then rub the nuts in a dish towel to remove the skins.

3 Place the water in a heavy pan and add the sugar. Add the cream of tartar, then heat gently to dissolve, stirring occasionally. Once the sugar has dissolved, do not stir the mixture. Turn the heat up to high and bring the mixture to the boil. Boil the syrup, without stirring, until it caramelizes slightly and is a light golden colour.

4 Carefully pour the caramel over the toasted hazelnuts on the baking sheet. Leave it to set. Once the caramel has set, break the slab into pieces, then blitz to a fine powder in a food processor.

5 Gently heat the cream in a pan until it is just below boiling. Meanwhile, place the butter and chopped chocolate in a heatproof bowl. Pour the cream over the chocolate and whisk gently until the chocolate has melted. Fold in the ground hazelnut powder. Pour the mixture into the prepared tin (pan) and chill for about 1 hour, until set. Turn the chocolate out on to a cold, hard surface and slice the block into 2cm/¾in squares.

6 Place the chocolate squares back in the refrigerator to chill for a further 30 minutes. The next step requires your tempered milk chocolate, so prepare it now. Line a baking sheet with baking parchment.

7 Following the instructions on page 17 dip the squares of ganache into the tempered milk chocolate using a dipping fork, and place on the baking parchment. Leave for about 30 minutes, or until completely set.

Energy 75kcal/315kJ; Protein 1g; Carbohydrate 7g, of which sugars 7g; Fat 5g, of which saturates 3g; Cholesterol 4mg; Calcium 16mg; Fibre 0g; Sodium 5mg

Ceylon Cinnamon Truffles

The combination of chocolate and cinnamon is a classic one, and the union is delicious. Ceylon cinnamon is readily available, but you will need to grind it yourself in a coffee grinder or with a mortar and pestle. The flavour will also be much fresher if you do this.

Makes about 100

200ml/7fl oz/scant 1 cup double (heavy) cream

100ml/3½fl oz/scant ½ cup liquid glucose

2 Ceylon cinnamon sticks, snapped in half

300g/11oz dark (bittersweet) chocolate (70% cocoa solids), chopped

100g/3¾oz/scant ½ cup unsalted butter, softened

400g/14oz dark (bittersweet) chocolate (70% cocoa solids), tempered (see pages 12–13)

400g/14oz milk chocolate (40% cocoa solids), tempered (see pages 12–13)

freshly ground Ceylon cinnamon, for sprinkling

1 Line a baking sheet with baking parchment and set aside. Place the cream and liquid glucose in a small pan. Add the cinnamon sticks to the pan. Bring to just under the boil and stir to blend in the glucose, then remove from the heat. Cover with a lid and leave to steep for 15 minutes.

2 Place the pan back over the heat, remove the lid and bring the cream mixture to just under the boil again. Place the chopped dark chocolate in a large heatproof bowl and pour in the hot cream mixture through a fine-mesh sieve (strainer). Discard the cinnamon sticks. Stand for 10 minutes.

3 Following the instructions on pages 14–15 add the butter to the combined chocolate and cream mixture to form a smooth, creamy ganache. Create ganache truffles as instructed on page 15. Prepare the tempered dark chocolate while the ganache is chilling.

4 Dip each truffle into the tempered dark chocolate and place on the baking sheet. Set for 15 minutes while you temper the milk chocolate. Dip each truffle into the tempered milk chocolate. Place it back on the baking sheet. Set for 30 minutes then sprinkle each truffle with ground cinnamon.

Energy 155kcal/647kJ; Protein 1g; Carbohydrate 15g, of which sugars 14g; Fat 10g, of which saturates 6g; Cholesterol 11mg; Calcium 29mg; Fibre 0g; Sodium 14mg

White Chocolate Espresso Truffles

The combination of white and dark chocolate, and silky coffee-flavoured truffle, is absolutely delicious in these treats. The dark chocolate will show through the final white chocolate layer of the truffle, but that is intentional and looks fabulous when you bite or cut into them.

Makes about 100

250ml/8fl oz/1 cup double (heavy) cream
50g/2oz/½ cup whole espresso beans
400g/14oz white chocolate, chopped
15ml/1 tbsp brandy
300g/11oz dark (bittersweet) chocolate (70% cocoa solids), tempered (see page 12–13)
550g/1lb 4oz white chocolate, tempered (see page 12–13)
10g/¼oz espresso beans, very finely ground

Cook's Tip

When making the ganache take care not to overmix it, as the white chocolate can seize up.

1 Line a baking sheet with baking parchment and set aside. Place the cream and espresso beans in a small pan over moderate heat and bring to just under the boil. Remove from the heat and allow the beans to steep for 10 minutes, then heat the mixture to just under the boil again.

2 Place the chopped white chocolate in a heatproof bowl and, holding a fine-mesh sieve (strainer) above it to catch the espresso beans, pour in the hot cream. Discard the espresso beans. Add the brandy and leave to cool. When the mixture is cool and the chocolate looks melted, whisk to form a smooth, creamy ganache. Leave for 15 minutes to begin to firm and then pipe into even blobs following the instructions on page 15.

3 For the next stage, you will need the tempered dark chocolate, so you can prepare it while the ganache is chilling. Dip each ball of ganache into the tempered dark chocolate, and place it back on the baking sheet.

4 Leave to set for 15 minutes while you temper the white chocolate. Dip each truffle into the tempered white chocolate. Place on the baking sheet and leave to set for 30 minutes. Sprinkle with ground espresso beans.

Energy 155kcal/647kJ; Protein 1.9g; Carbohydrate 15.1g, of which sugars 14.8g; Fat 10.3g, of which saturates 6g; Cholesterol 7mg; Calcium 56mg; Fibre 0g; Sodium 23mg

Champagne Truffles

A version of this traditional classic is made by almost every good chocolatier. You could make them with any sparkling wine that you like to drink, such as prosecco or cava, instead of Champagne. Rosé Champagne makes an especially delicious truffle.

Makes about 100

250g/9oz dark (bittersweet) chocolate (70% cocoa solids), chopped

200g/7oz milk chocolate (40% cocoa solids), chopped

150ml/¼ pint/⅔ cup double (heavy) cream

50g/2oz/¼ cup unsalted butter, plus extra for greasing

100ml/3½fl oz/scant ½ cup Champagne or other sparkling wine

15ml/1 tbsp brandy

700g/1lb 10oz dark chocolate (70% cocoa solids), tempered (see pages 12–13)

unsweetened cocoa powder, for dusting, and icing (confectioners') sugar, for rolling

edible gold dust (optional)

1 Grease a 20cm/8in square baking tin (pan) and line with clear film (plastic wrap). Line a baking sheet with baking parchment. Put the chopped dark and milk chocolate in a heatproof bowl. Set aside.

2 Put the cream and butter in a small, heavy pan and heat to just under a boil over moderate heat. Swirl the cream around occasionally so that it does not burn around the edges of the pan.

3 Pour the heated cream over the chopped chocolate and let it sit for about 1 minute before adding the Champagne and brandy. Whisk by hand until all the chocolate is melted and you have a smooth ganache. Pour the mixture into the prepared tin and leave until the mixture begins to firm up.

4 Pipe the ganache into truffles following the instructions on page 15.

5 Dust your palms with cocoa powder and roll the ganache blobs into balls. Return these to the refrigerator for 10 minutes, until firm. For the next stage, you will need your tempered chocolate, so you can prepare it while the ganache is chilling.

6 Place a wire rack on the work surface with a sheet of baking parchment underneath to catch the drips. Dip each ball of ganache into the tempered dark chocolate and then place on a wire rack to set.

7 Place the icing sugar in a small bowl and roll the truffles in it to coat. Roll the truffles in edible gold dust, if using. Alternatively, dip a clean, dry pastry brush into the gold dust, hold it over the truffles and tap the handle of the pastry brush. Leave to set for about 30 minutes.

8 Serve immediately or store the truffles in the refrigerator in an airtight container, spaced well apart.

Energy 144kcal/601kJ; Protein 1.3g; Carbohydrate 14.8g, of which sugars 13.7g; Fat 9.2g, of which saturates 5.4g; Cholesterol 9mg; Calcium 18mg; Fibre 0g; Sodium 16mg

Grand Marnier Chocolate Truffles

These adult treats contain the classic combination of Grand Marnier and dark chocolate. Finishing the truffles by rolling them in chopped candied orange peel adds both texture and additional flavour, as well as making them even prettier.

Makes about 100

120ml/4fl oz/½ cup double (heavy) cream

100ml/3¾ fl oz/scant ½ cup golden (light corn) syrup

1 vanilla pod (bean), split in half

350g/12oz dark (bittersweet) chocolate (66–70% cocoa solids), chopped

50g/2oz/¼ cup unsalted butter, softened (it needs to be very soft)

10ml/2 tsp Grand Marnier

100g/3¾oz/⅔ cup candied orange peel, chopped and tossed in caster (superfine) sugar

1 Stir the cream and golden syrup together in a heavy pan, then scrape the vanilla seeds out of the pod and add to the pan along with the pod. Warm over a low heat and bring to just below the boil. Remove from the heat, transfer to a large heatproof mixing bowl and cover with clear film (plastic wrap). Chill overnight for optimum vanilla flavour.

2 Grease a 20cm/8in square baking tin (pan) and line with clear film (plastic wrap). Place the chocolate in a heatproof bowl and set it over a pan of barely simmering water. Using a chocolate thermometer, heat the chocolate to just below 46°C/115°F. Remove from the heat.

3 Meanwhile, place the bowl containing the cream and golden syrup mixture over a pan of simmering water, remove and discard the vanilla pod, then heat the cream mixture to just below 46°C/115°F.

4 Once they have both reached the desired temperature, pour the melted chocolate and the heated cream into a blender, and blend until it is thick and creamy. Add the very soft butter, bit by bit, blending well between each addition. Add the Grand Marnier and blend.

5 Pour the ganache into the prepared baking tin and smooth the surface. Leave to cool for a few hours until it has set.

6 Form smooth round truffles following the instructions on page 16. Roll each ball in the chopped candied orange peel and sugar mixture until they are fully coated.

7 Serve immediately, or place the truffles in a bag or container and store them in the refrigerator. This can cause the sugar on the candied peel to dissolve, so you will need to toss them in caster sugar again before serving.

Energy 66kcal/277kJ; Protein 0.4g; Carbohydrate 7.4g, of which sugars 7g; Fat 4.2g, of which saturates 2.5g; Cholesterol 6mg; Calcium 7mg; Fibre 0.1g; Sodium 20mg

Lavender-milk Chocolate Truffles

A plant with endless uses, lavender looks beautiful, smells wonderful and has relaxing and soothing properties. Its delicate taste is especially suited to sweet honey and creamy milk chocolate. An edible shimmery dust provides the perfect finishing touch to these truffles.

Makes about 100

200ml/7fl oz/scant 1 cup double (heavy) cream
80ml/5 tbsp liquid glucose
20ml/4 tsp honey
20ml/4 tsp dried edible lavender buds
300g/11oz dark (bittersweet) chocolate (64% cocoa solids), chopped
400g/14oz milk chocolate (40% cocoa solids), tempered (see pages 12–13)
purple and silver edible shimmery dust

1 Grease a 20cm/8in square baking tin (pan) and line with clear film (plastic wrap). Place the cream, liquid glucose and honey in a small pan. Bring to just under the boil and stir to blend in the glucose and honey. Add the lavender buds and remove from the heat. Cover and leave to steep for 15 minutes, then heat to just under the boil again.

2 Place the chopped dark chocolate in a heatproof bowl and, holding a fine-mesh sieve (strainer) above it to catch the lavender, pour in the hot cream. Discard the lavender. Leave for 10 minutes.

3 Following the instructions on pages 14–15 combine the chocolate and cream to form a smooth, creamy ganache. Pipe balls of truffles following the instructions on page 15. For the next stage, you will need the tempered milk chocolate, so you can prepare it while the ganache is chilling.

4 Roll each blob of chilled ganache into a ball. Then dip each ball into the tempered milk chocolate. Place on a wire rack. Dip a clean, dry pastry brush into the pot of purple or silver dust and carefully shake the brush over the truffles to release the dust. Leave to set for 30 minutes.

Energy 98kcal/411kJ; Protein 1g; Carbohydrate 10g, of which sugars 9g; Fat 6g, of which saturates 4g; Cholesterol 8mg; Calcium 22mg; Fibre 0g; Sodium 10mg

Rose and Violet Creams

Old-fashioned and classic, chocolate creams made with sweet, delicate floral essences are becoming popular once again. You can make the dainty crystallized rose petals and violets, or they can be found at speciality supermarkets and delicatessens.

Makes about 50

300g/11oz ready-made fondant
2–3 drops rose syrup
2–3 drops violet syrup
400g/14oz dark (bittersweet) chocolate (at least 70% cocoa solids), tempered (see pages 12–13)
crystallized rose petals
crystallized violets

1 Place a sheet of baking parchment underneath a wire rack.
2 Divide the fondant in half. Knead the rose syrup into one half of the fondant and knead the violet syrup into the other half. Roll them both into long, thin logs. Cut each log into 25 bitesize pieces and roll them into balls.
3 Temper the dark chocolate following the instructions on pages 12-13. Dip each ball of fondant into the tempered chocolate, using a dipping fork, then place on the wire rack.
4 Decorate the rose creams with the rose petals and the violet creams with the violets. Leave to set for 30 minutes. Serve immediately, or store in an airtight container, spaced apart, in the refrigerator. Remove 30 minutes before serving, as chocolate is best eaten at room temperature.

Cook's Tip
Ready-made fondant can be purchased from many supermarkets and specialist online cake decorating suppliers.

Energy 66kcal/278kJ; Protein 0.5g; Carbohydrate 10.5g, of which sugars 9.9g; Fat 2.8g, of which saturates 1.6g; Cholesterol 1mg; Calcium 6mg; Fibre 0g; Sodium 2mg

Cherry-Kirsch Truffles

Some people are not keen on commercial cherry-flavoured chocolates, but it is well worth trying these home-made ones, as they taste completely different. This classic recipe consists of a perfect cherry nestled in a Kirsch-spiked ganache, enrobed in intense dark chocolate.

Makes 30

500g/1¼lb dark (bittersweet) chocolate (61–64% cocoa solids), tempered (see pages 12–13)

40g/1½oz Amarena or other good quality sour cherries in syrup

15ml/1 tbsp Kirsch

90ml/6 tbsp double (heavy) cream

75g/3oz/¼ cup golden (light corn) syrup

100g/3¾oz dark (bittersweet) chocolate (70% cocoa solids), chopped

Cook's Tip

If the cherries are too large to fit in your chocolate mould, slice them and have just half a cherry in each one.

1 Line a baking sheet with baking parchment and set aside. Coat the cups of a chocolate mould tray with most of the tempered dark chocolate. (Leave enough to add a final layer later.) Hold the mould at an angle over a clean bowl so that the chocolate runs down, coating the cups, and any excess drizzles out into the bowl.

2 Tap on a work surface to release any bubbles. Lay the mould upside down on the baking sheet. After a few minutes, check the mould to see if the chocolate has begun to set on the sides.

3 Using the back of a sharp knife, scrape away any excess chocolate from the flat plastic surrounding the cups. Return the mould right side up to the baking sheet to allow the chocolate to set fully. This will take 1 hour.

4 Meanwhile, strain the cherries and reserve the syrup. Put 60ml/4 tbsp of the syrup in a small bowl and stir in the Kirsch. Set aside.

5 Make the ganache. Place the cream and syrup in a small pan and bring to the boil. Melt the chopped chocolate in a heatproof bowl set over a pan of barely simmering water. Pour the cream over the chocolate and, using a whisk, blend into a ganache. Add the reserved cherry syrup and mix again. Leave it to cool to 29°C/85°F on a sugar thermometer.

6 Transfer the ganache to a squeeze bottle and half-fill each chocolate cup with the ganache. Push a cherry into the centre of the ganache in each cup. Fill the cups almost to the top with more ganache.

7 Cover the ganache with a layer of the remaining tempered chocolate. Scrape any excess chocolate off the top with an offset spatula, and leave to set for 1 hour. Invert the mould and tap lightly to remove the chocolates.

Energy 136kcal/569kJ; Protein 1g; Carbohydrate 15g, of which sugars 15g; Fat 8g, of which saturates 5g; Cholesterol 6mg; Calcium 9mg; Fibre 0g; Sodium 2mg

Salted Caramel Chocolates

These elegant chocolates consist of a dark caramel and sea salt ganache, coated with a layer of yet more dark chocolate. Salt and caramel make a wonderful combination, and they have been used together in confectionery for many years.

Makes about 100

50ml/2fl oz/¼ cup cold water
200g/7oz/1 cup caster (superfine) sugar
2.5ml/½ tsp cream of tartar
225ml/8fl oz/scant 1 cup double (heavy) cream
50g/2oz/¼ cup unsalted butter, plus extra for greasing
2.5ml/½ tsp sea salt, crushed, plus extra to decorate
425g/15oz dark (bittersweet) chocolate (70% cocoa solids), finely chopped
400g/14oz dark chocolate (61–64% cocoa solids), tempered (see pages 12–13)

1 Grease a 20cm/8in square cake tin (pan), and line with clear film (plastic wrap). Line a baking sheet with baking parchment. Place the water in a pan, add the sugar and cream of tartar and heat gently to dissolve, stirring.
2 Once the sugar has dissolved, bring it to the boil and boil until the syrup caramelizes. Do not allow it to burn. Slowly and very carefully add the cream (it will spatter, so use caution and wear oven gloves). Use a whisk to incorporate it fully. Add the butter and salt, and whisk until smooth.
3 Put the chopped dark chocolate in a large, heatproof bowl. Pour in the caramel mixture and, following the instructions on page 14–15 combine the caramel and chocolate into a smooth, creamy ganache and pour into the square cake tin and leave to set.
4 When the ganache is set, cut square truffles following the instructions on page 17. Meanwhile, temper the remaining dark chocolate.
5 Dip the chilled squares in the melted chocolate and transfer them to the baking sheet. Sprinkle with sea salt. Leave to set for about 30 minutes. Serve as they are or in individual paper or foil cups.

Energy 130kcal/543kJ; Protein 0.9g; Carbohydrate 15g, of which sugars 14.1g; Fat 8.1g, of which saturates 4.7g; Cholesterol 10mg; Calcium 11mg; Fibre 0g; Sodium 11mg

Grapefruit and Pink Pepper Truffles

Although grapefruit can be sour, it is fabulous when served in combination with chocolate. The bitterness of the dark chocolate emphasizes the sweet notes of the fruit, bringing out its fresh flavour, while infusing the cream with pink peppercorns adds a subtle spicy note.

Makes about 100

200ml/7fl oz/scant 1 cup double (heavy) cream
100ml/3½fl oz/scant ½ cup liquid glucose or golden (light corn) syrup
grated rind of 2 grapefruits
5ml/1 tsp whole pink peppercorns, plus extra crushed peppercorns for decoration
300g/11oz dark (bittersweet) chocolate (70% cocoa solids), chopped
100g/3¾oz/scant ½ cup unsalted butter, softened, plus extra for greasing
400g/14oz dark chocolate (61–64% cocoa solids), tempered (see pages 12–13)
50g/2oz/⅓ cup candied grapefruit or citron peel, finely chopped

1 Grease a 20cm/8in square cake tin (pan), then line with clear film (plastic wrap). Line a baking sheet with baking parchment. Place the cream, liquid glucose or golden syrup, and grapefruit rind in a pan. Heat gently and bring to just under the boil, stirring, then stir in the peppercorns. Remove from the heat. Cover and leave to steep for 15 minutes.

2 Put the chopped dark chocolate in a heatproof bowl. Heat the cream once again to just under the boil and pour through a fine-mesh sieve (strainer) into the bowl containing the chocolate. Stand for 10 minutes.

3 Following the instructions on pages 14–15 add the butter to the chocolate and cream mixture to form a smooth ganache. Allow to set.

4 When set, cut into square truffles following the instructions on page 17. Meanwhile, temper the dark chocolate.

5 Dip the squares of ganache into the tempered chocolate and place them on the baking sheet. Decorate with crushed pink peppercorns and candied grapefruit peel. Leave for about 30 minutes to set completely.

Energy 57kcal/239kJ; Protein 0g; Carbohydrate 6g, of which sugars 6g; Fat 4g, of which saturates 2g; Cholesterol 5mg; Calcium 4mg; Fibre 0g; Sodium 5mg

Crystallized Ginger Chocolates

Ginger and dark chocolate complement each other very well, creating a grown-up flavour combination that is deep and intense. Fresh root ginger is added to the ganache in this recipe, giving it a fiery taste, while candied ginger adds a sweet yet peppery note.

Makes about 50

200ml/7fl oz/scant 1 cup double (heavy) cream
100ml/3½fl oz/scant ½ cup liquid glucose or golden (light corn) syrup
50g/2oz fresh root ginger, chopped
300g/11oz dark (bittersweet) chocolate (70% cocoa solids), chopped
100g/3¾oz/scant ½ cup unsalted butter, softened, plus extra for greasing
400g/14oz dark chocolate (61–64% cocoa solids), tempered (see pages 12–13)
50g/2oz candied ginger, chopped in 5mm/¼in pieces

1 Grease a 20cm/8in square cake tin (pan), then line with clear film (plastic wrap). Line a baking sheet with baking parchment. Place the cream, liquid glucose or golden syrup and fresh ginger in a small pan. Heat gently and bring to just under the boil, stirring well, then remove from the heat. Cover and leave to steep for 15 minutes.

2 Put the chopped dark chocolate in a heatproof bowl. Heat the cream once again to just under the boil and pour through a fine-mesh sieve (strainer) into the bowl containing the chocolate. Stand for 10 minutes.

3 Following the instructions on pages 14–15 add the butter to the chocolate and cream mixture to form a smooth ganache. Allow to set.

4 When set, cut into square truffles following the instructions on page 17. Cut each square in half diagonally to make triangles. Chill for a further 30 minutes. Temper the dark chocolate while the ganache is chilling.

5 Dip the triangles of ganache into the tempered chocolate and place on the baking sheet. Place a piece of candied ginger on each. Leave for about 30 minutes, until completely set.

Energy 57kcal/240kJ; Protein 1g; Carbohydrate 6g, of which sugars 5g; Fat 4g, of which saturates 2g; Cholesterol 5mg; Calcium 4mg; Fibre 0g; Sodium 5mg

Chocolate Boats

Buttery sweet shortcrust pastry boats are the perfect vehicle for rich, dark chocolate ganache. You can prepare the pastry shells in advance, then simply create the ganache at the last minute, to make easy and elegant petits fours. You will need some small boat moulds.

Makes about 24

115g/4oz/½ cup unsalted butter, softened
50g/2oz/¼ cup caster (superfine) sugar
175g/6oz/1½ cups plain (all-purpose) flour, plus extra for dusting
a pinch of salt
½ egg yolk
175g/6oz dark (bittersweet) chocolate (64–70% cocoa solids), finely chopped
60ml/4 tbsp/¼ cup double (heavy) cream
50g/2oz/4 tbsp unsalted butter, softened (it needs to be very soft)

1　To make the pastry, cream the butter and sugar together until light but not too fluffy. Add the flour and salt, and mix until combined. Add the egg yolk and bring together into a ball. Wrap the ball in clear film (plastic wrap) and chill in the refrigerator for about 30 minutes, until firm but not hard.

2　Lightly dust a worktop and the dough with flour. Roll out the dough to about 3mm/⅛ in thickness. The pastry boats need to be strong enough to stand on their own, but not so thick that they dominate the chocolate.

3　Cut teardrop shapes that are slightly larger than the moulds. Use a knife to lift them gently off the worktop and into the moulds. Press them into place and trim off any excess. Place them on a baking sheet. Chill for 15 minutes. Meanwhile, preheat the oven to 180°C/350°F/Gas 4.

4　Bake the pastry shells for 7 minutes, or until they are just golden at the edges and are baked through. Leave to cook, then remove from the moulds and transfer to a serving tray.

5　Make the ganache, following the instructions on pages 14–15. Before the ganache sets, spoon the mixture into the pastry shells and serve.

Energy 126kcal/526kJ; Protein 1.2g; Carbohydrate 14.4g, of which sugars 7.5g; Fat 7.6g, of which saturates 4.6g; Cholesterol 19mg; Calcium 17mg; Fibre 0.2g; Sodium 41mg

Mint Meltaways

A meltaway centre is different from a ganache one, because it uses coconut oil or cocoa butter instead of cream. This creates a silky texture that melts in your mouth very quickly. Once mixed with chocolate, the flavour of coconut oil is undetectable.

Makes 50–100

115g/4oz coconut oil
450g/1lb dark (bittersweet) chocolate (at least 60% cocoa solids), chopped
2.5ml/½ tsp peppermint extract
250g/9oz dark chocolate (at least 60% cocoa solids), tempered (see pages 12–13)
green or silver sugar balls

1 Line a 15cm/6in or 20cm/8in square cake tin (pan) with baking parchment. The size of tin you choose depends on how thick or thin you want the meltaways to be – a smaller tin will create a thicker confection.

2 Melt the coconut oil very gently in a large heatproof bowl set over a pan of simmering water. Use a sugar thermometer to ensure it does not rise above 24°C/74°F. Whisk in the chopped chocolate until smooth. Stir in the peppermint extract. Pour the mixture into the prepared tin and chill in the refrigerator for 30 minutes, until set.

3 Turn the set mixture out on to a marble slab or other cold, hard surface. Dip a large knife in hot water, wipe it dry and use it to slice the block into 2cm/¾in squares. Chill the pieces again for 10 minutes. Meanwhile, temper the remaining dark chocolate.

4 Dip the peppermint pieces into the tempered chocolate and transfer to a clean sheet of baking parchment. Decorate with a drizzle of tempered chocolate and add a green or silver ball immediately. Leave to set for 30 minutes before serving.

Cook's Tip

Do not overheat the coconut oil as it can burn the chocolate and result in a grainy texture.

Energy 46kcal/192kJ; Protein 0g; Carbohydrate 4g, of which sugars 4g; Fat 3g, of which saturates 2g; Cholesterol 0mg; Calcium 2mg; Fibre 0g; Sodium 0mg

Chocolate Raspberry Meltaways

These soft, velvety meltaways are made with a fruity, fresh raspberry purée that brings out the flavour of the dark chocolate. Drizzled with milk chocolate and dusted with edible pink dust, they are extremely attractive and would make an ideal gift.

Makes 50–100

115g/4oz coconut oil
400g/14oz dark (bittersweet) chocolate (at least 60% cocoa solids), chopped
100g/3¾oz/1¼ cups puréed raspberries, strained (made from 200g/7oz/2 cups whole berries)
250g/9oz dark chocolate (at least 60% cocoa solids), tempered (see pages 12–13)
100g/3¾oz milk chocolate, tempered (see pages 12–13)
edible pink dust or silver balls

1 Line a 15cm/6in or 20cm/8in square cake tin (pan) with baking parchment, depending on how thick or thin you want the meltaways to be – a smaller tin will give a thicker confection.

2 Melt the coconut oil very gently in a large heatproof bowl positioned over a pan of simmering water. Use a sugar thermometer to ensure that it does not rise above 24°C/74°F. Whisk in the chopped chocolate until smooth. Stir in the raspberry purée. Pour the mixture into the tin. Chill in the refrigerator for 30 minutes, until set.

3 Turn the set mixture out on to a marble slab or other cold, hard surface. Dip a knife in hot water, wipe it dry and use it to slice the block into 2cm/¾in squares. Chill the pieces again for 10 minutes. Meanwhile, temper the remaining dark chocolate and the milk chocolate.

4 Dip the raspberry pieces into the tempered dark chocolate and transfer to a clean sheet of baking parchment. Decorate with a drizzle of tempered milk chocolate and use a clean, dry pastry brush to sprinkle the tops with edible pink dust, or add silver balls. Leave to set for 30 minutes.

Cook's Tip
Coconut oil is solid at room temperature, but it is very soft.

Energy 49kcal/204kJ; Protein 0g; Carbohydrate 5g, of which sugars 5g; Fat 3g, of which saturates 2g; Cholesterol 1mg; Calcium 5mg; Fibre 0g; Sodium 1mg

Chocolate Peppermint Creams

Junior Mints, Peppermint Patties and After Eight Mints are all inspirations for these little chocolate treats. They are very easy to make and delicious to eat. The darker the chocolate the better, as this provides the best contrast to the strong peppermint fondant.

Makes about 80

2–3 drops peppermint oil
300g/11oz ready-made fondant
400g/14oz dark (bittersweet) chocolate (at least 70% cocoa solids)

1 Line a baking sheet with baking parchment or place a sheet of baking parchment under a wire rack.

2 Knead the peppermint oil into the fondant and divide the mixture into 4 pieces. Roll into 4 logs.

3 Cut each log into about 20 bitesize pieces and either flatten them into discs using the flat edge of a knife or roll into balls and then flatten them with your hands. Meanwhile temper the chocolate, following the instructions on pages 12–13.

4 Dip each disc of peppermint fondant into the tempered chocolate using a dipping fork. Place on the baking parchment or cooling rack and leave for about 30 minutes, until completely set.

5 Serve immediately, or store in an airtight container in the refrigerator for up to 1 week.

Variation
If you prefer, flavour the fondant with a few drops of orange or strawberry essence.

Energy 26kcal/107kJ; Protein 0g; Carbohydrate 3g, of which sugars 3g; Fat 1g, of which saturates 1g; Cholesterol 0mg; Calcium 2mg; Fibre 0g; Sodium 0mg

Chocolate Lips and Hearts

Lips and hearts are appropriate shapes for these rich, intense chocolates, which are perfect for a romantic dinner. They are quite fiddly to make but the results are impressive – the trick is to make the chocolate shell just thick enough to contain the runny caramel.

Makes about 25

300g/11oz/1½ cups caster (superfine) sugar

50ml/2fl oz/¼ cup water

1 vanilla pod (bean), split and seeds scraped

175ml/6fl oz/¾ cup double (heavy) cream

45ml/3 tbsp golden (light corn) syrup

90g/3½oz/⅓ cup unsalted butter, softened

a pinch of salt

edible gold leaf (optional)

white chocolate, tempered (see pages 12-13), for drizzling (optional)

500g/1¼lb dark (bittersweet) chocolate (at least 64% cocoa solids), tempered (see pages 12-13)

1　Line a shallow baking tray with baking parchment and set it aside. Put the sugar and water into a large, heavy pan and heat gently, stirring, until the sugar has dissolved. Once it has dissolved, stop stirring. Add the scraped vanilla seeds and the pod. Continue to cook until the sugar syrup is a dark caramel colour, but be careful not to let it burn. (As soon as you see the first wisp of smoke, it is done.) Meanwhile, while the caramel is cooking, pour the cream and golden syrup into a small pan and bring to the boil. Keep your eye on the caramel too.

2　When the caramel is ready, remove it from the heat. Slowly pour the cream mixture into it, taking great care that you do not burn your hand from the spattering of the caramel or the steam. Use a whisk to mix and release more of the steam and dissipate the bubbles. Stir in the butter and salt, and remove the vanilla pod. Insert a sugar thermometer and let the caramel cool to 27°C/80°F. This can take a couple of hours. When it has cooled, pour it into a squeeze bottle and set aside.

3　If you want to decorate the outside of the chocolates, place small pieces of gold leaf inside the cups of a chocolate heart mould and drizzle tempered white chocolate in lip-shaped ones. Let the white chocolate set a little, then scrape away any excess on the mould.

4　Coat the cups with most of the tempered dark chocolate. Hold the mould at an angle over a clean bowl so that the chocolate runs down and coats the inside of the cups. Tap on a work surface to release any bubbles. Lay the mould upside down on the baking sheet. After a few minutes check the mould to see if the chocolate has begun to set on the sides.

Energy 83kcal/349kJ; Protein 0.2g; Carbohydrate 13.8g, of which sugars 13.8g; Fat 3.8g, of which saturates 2.1g; Cholesterol 9mg; Calcium 10mg; Fibre 0g; Sodium 7mg

5 Scrape away any excess chocolate from the flat plastic surrounding the lip and heart cups and allow to set completely. This will take about 1 hour.

6 When the filling is cool enough and the chocolate has set, fill the cups with the caramel, using the squeeze bottle. Tap on a surface to release any bubbles and leave them, uncovered, overnight.

7 The next day, temper a little more dark chocolate and pour over the set caramel filling. Scrape any excess chocolate off the top (which will be the bottom of the chocolates) with a spatula. Leave to set for 1–1½ hours.

8 Invert the moulds and tap lightly to remove the chocolates.

Cook's Tip
The key to these chocolates is to make the shell just thick enough to contain the runny caramel, as a too-thick shell ruins the delicacy of the truffle.

Peanut Butter Cups

The silky texture of the peanut butter ganache inside a crisp milk chocolate shell is truly scrumptious. Although tempering chocolate will give the best results, you could just melt the chocolate and not temper it if you want to make these with children or you are short of time.

Makes 18

250g/9oz milk chocolate,
 tempered (see pages 12–13)
115g/4oz milk chocolate, finely
 chopped
100g/3¾oz/scant ½ cup smooth
 peanut butter
sea salt

1 Set out 18 mini cupcake liners, then put another 18 inside them so they are double thickness. Using a clean brush, paint the insides with a generous layer of tempered milk chocolate, reserving about 100g/3¾oz for the tops. Set them aside to set for 20 minutes.

2 Put the chopped chocolate in a heatproof bowl over a pan of barely simmering water and leave to melt. Stir in the peanut butter. Remove from the heat and leave the mixture to cool to 29°C/85°F. (It needs to be this cool or it will melt the cups when you fill them.)

3 Transfer the ganache to a squeeze bottle and three-quarter fill the chocolate cups with it. Chill them in the refrigerator for 20 minutes to set the filling.

4 Meanwhile, check that the rest of the tempered chocolate is still at the right temperature, or temper a little more milk chocolate. Remove the cups from the refrigerator and top with the rest of the tempered chocolate. It is easiest to do this using a squeeze bottle. Sprinkle the tops with a little salt. Leave to set for 20 minutes before serving.

Cook's Tip
It is well worth paying a little extra to buy an organic peanut butter, as the flavour will be much better.

Energy 138kcal/575kJ; Protein 2g; Carbohydrate 13g, of which sugars 13g; Fat 9g, of which saturates 4g; Cholesterol 2mg; Calcium 21mg; Fibre 0g; Sodium 47mg

White and Dark Chocolate Bark

Chocolate barks are essentially sophisticated chocolate bars: the best way to enjoy a good quality chocolate with a little extra embellishment. This recipe is very easy to make and the addition of crunchy sea salt is reminiscent of chocolate-covered pretzels.

Makes about 550g/1lb 4oz

50g/2oz dark (bittersweet) chocolate (70% cocoa solids)
500g/1¼lb white chocolate, finely chopped
5ml/1 tsp flaky sea salt

1 Line a baking tray with baking parchment and set aside. Chop the dark chocolate into fine shards.

2 Place the white chocolate in a heatproof bowl positioned over a pan of barely simmering water. Do not let the water touch the bottom of the bowl or the chocolate will burn. Stir occasionally to assist the melting.

3 Pour two-thirds of the melted white chocolate into the prepared baking tray and spread it evenly using an offset metal spatula. Sprinkle with the salt, then sprinkle with the finely chopped dark chocolate.

4 Pour the remaining white chocolate on the top. Smooth it with an offset spatula and leave to set for 12–15 minutes.

5 Remove the chocolate from the baking tray. Place a cutting board on top of it and invert the bark. Pull off the parchment paper. Cut the bark into irregular pieces with a sharp knife.

6 Serve immediately or store the pieces of bark in an airtight container, spaced well apart, in the refrigerator.

Cook's Tip

Bark makes a great gift. Simply break the sheet up into big pieces and wrap them individually in baking parchment or waxed paper to stop any cocoa butter seeping through, then finish them with wrapping paper and a ribbon.

Energy 2908kcal/12159kJ; Protein 42.4g; Carbohydrate 323.9g, of which sugars 321.3g; Fat 169.1g, of which saturates 99.5g; Cholesterol 5mg; Calcium 1370mg; Fibre 0g; Sodium 2521mg

Milk Chocolate and Macadamia Nut Bark

You could use any of your favourite nuts here, but the macadamia works very well, especially with the buttery crunchy coating they have when caramelized. A sprinkling of salt adds an extra dimension to the chocolate and nut flavour combination.

Makes about 1kg/2¼ lb

200g/7oz/1 cup caster (superfine) sugar
100g/3¾oz/scant ½ cup unsalted butter
250g/9oz macadamia nuts, chopped
500g/1¼lb milk chocolate (40% cocoa solids)
5ml/1 tsp flaky sea salt

Cook's Tip
Use the best-quality sea salt that you can find, such as Maldon or fleur de sel.

1 Line two baking trays with baking parchment and set aside.
2 Put the sugar and half of the butter in a small pan and warm over a medium heat until the butter starts to bubble. Add the chopped macadamia nuts and, using a wooden spoon, stir constantly until coated. Stir in the remaining butter, then remove from the heat.
3 Spread the nuts out on one of the baking trays and leave to cool.
4 Place the milk chocolate in a heatproof bowl and set over a pan of barely simmering water. Do not let the water touch the bottom of the bowl. Pour the melted chocolate into the other prepared baking tray. Spread the chocolate evenly with an offset spatula to about 5mm/¼in thick.
5 Sprinkle over the salt, then sprinkle the caramelized nuts on top. Leave to set for 12–15 minutes.
6 Remove the chocolate from the tray by sliding the baking parchment on to a chopping board. Slide an offset spatula between the chocolate and the paper and pull the paper away. Cut the bark into irregular pieces with a sharp knife. Serve immediately or store in an airtight container.

Energy 5378kcal/22437kJ; Protein 60g; Carbohydrate 514g, of which sugars 512g; Fat 357g, of which saturates 125g; Cholesterol 23mg; Calcium 1490mg; Fibre 0g; Sodium 3228mg

Flaked Almond Bark

This is one of the easiest chocolate treats you can make, and it is extremely versatile. This recipe is for a bark made with flaked almonds suspended in dark chocolate and topped with pistachios, but you could use whichever combination of chocolate type and nuts you prefer.

Makes about 450g/1lb

200g/7oz/scant 2 cups flaked (sliced) almonds
200g/7oz dark (bittersweet) chocolate (55%–64% cocoa solids)
50g/2oz/½ cup chopped pistachio nuts

1 Line a baking tray with clear film (plastic wrap) and set aside. Preheat the oven to 160°C/325°F/Gas 3.

2 Spread the nuts out on another baking sheet and place in the heated oven until just toasted. This should take about 7 minutes, depending on your oven. Watch them closely so they do not burn and go bitter.

3 Melt the dark chocolate in a heatproof bowl set over a pan of barely simmering water. Stir it occasionally to help it melt.

4 Add the warm, toasted almonds to the chocolate and stir to combine. Quickly scrape the mixture into the lined baking tray and smooth the surface. Tap the tray on the surface a few times to release any air bubbles.

5 Sprinkle the chopped pistachio nuts on top. Leave for 12–15 minutes to set. Alternatively, chill it in the refrigerator.

6 Lift the bark up by the edges of the clear film, gently lean the pistachio side against your fingertips and peel away the clear film with the other hand. Cut the bark into irregular pieces using a sharp knife.

Variation
Replace the almonds with chopped walnuts and coat with finely chopped candied fruit.

Energy 2575kcal/10705kJ; Protein 60.6g; Carbohydrate 147.5g, of which sugars 130.3g; Fat 197.7g, of which saturates 46.9g; Cholesterol 18mg; Calcium 611mg; Fibre 17.9g; Sodium 315mg

Index